Left or Right

by Wiley Blevins

CAPSTONE PRESS
a capstone imprint

Little Pebble is published by Pebble
1710 Roe Crest Drive, North Mankato,
Minnesota 56003
www.mycapstone.com

Library of Congress Cataloging-in-Publication Data
Library of Congress Cataloging-in-Publication Data is
available on the Library of Congress website.
ISBN 978-1-9771-0315-4 (library binding)
ISBN 978-1-9771-0541-7 (paperback)
ISBN 978-1-9771-0323-9 (ebook pdf)

Editorial Credits
Erika L. Shores, editor; Elyse White, designer;
Tracy Cummins, media researcher; Tori Abraham,
production specialist

Photo Credits
iStockphoto: FatCamera, Cover; Shutterstock: Africa
Studio, 17, Artazum, Cover Background, grafxart, 5,
kaesanr, 19, LightField Studios, 9, MommaAbbott,
Design Element, Monkey Business Images, 11, 13,
MyPhoto studio, 15, Photographee.eu, 7, photolinc,
Design Element, wavebreakmedia, 21

Printed and bound in China.
966

Table of Contents

Where Is It?. 4

At Home 6

At School. 14

    Glossary. 22
    Read More. 23
    Internet Sites 23
    Critical Thinking Questions . . . 24
    Index. 24

Where Is It?

Look around.

What do you see?

The red door is on the left.

The yellow door is on the right.

At Home

It's time to sleep.

The bed is on the right.

Hop in!

Good morning!

It's time for a hug.

The girl on the left smiles.

It's time to eat.

Dad watches on the left.

Crack!

They cook eggs.

It's time to go to school.

The boy is on the right.

His dad walks on the left.

At School

It's time for art.

Grab the purple scissors.

They are on the left.

It's time for lunch.

Use a fork.

It's on the right.

It's time for recess.

Go down the metal slide.

It's on the left.

Whee!

It's time to go home.

Line up on the right.

Then hop on the bus!

Glossary

metal—a hard, shiny material

recess—a short time during the school day when children can play

scissors—a tool used to cut paper and cloth

slide—a smooth piece of playground equipment on which children can easily move from the top to the bottom

Read More

Berne, Emma Carlson. *My School, Your School, Our Schools.* How We Are Alike and Different. North Mankato, Minn.: Cantata Learning, 2019.

Butterfield, Moira. *Homes Around the World.* Children Like Us. New York: Cavendish Square, 2016.

Internet Sites

Use FactHound to find Internet sites related to this book.

Visit www.facthound.com

Just type in 9781977103154 and go.

Check out projects, games and lots more at
www.capstonekids.com

Critical Thinking Questions

1. Describe ways children get to and from school.

2. What makes a healthy school lunch?

Index

art, 14

beds, 6

buses, 20

cooking, 10

doors, 4

eating, 10

homes, 20

lunch, 16

morning, 8

recess, 18

scissors, 14

walking, 12